# HE LOST HIS BABY TOO

## Survival Guide For The Grieving Dad

MISCARRIAGE—STILLBIRTH—INFANT DEATH

Kelly Farley
With David Dicola

ISBN-13: 978-0-9852051-2-6

Grieving Dads, Aurora, Illinois

# TABLE OF CONTENTS

# LETTER TO THE GRIEVING DAD

*Dear Dad,*

*You are reading this because something bad has happened. Something so gut-wrenching that it's impossible to put into words. As someone who has experienced similar losses, I understand the pain and sorrow you feel. It's extremely important that you understand and believe that no matter what has happened, you are still a dad. Nothing can take that away from you. Nothing.*

*I am deeply sorry for your loss and your need for this book, but it was written with you in mind. My hope is that what you are about to read will provide insight into your new reality. The reality that you, too, lost a baby and you will have to fight your way through the fog of grief setting in. This fight will challenge you and force you to see things in a different way than you may have up until this point in your life.*

*There is no doubt you feel or will feel broken at some point along this journey. We all feel like we've been broken into a million pieces at some point. However, it's important for you to understand that you are not broken beyond repair. Each chapter of this book was designed to help you process the grief and sorrow you will undoubtedly experience. It was developed to take those broken pieces and put them back together into the new you.*

*My goal is to help you through this pain, so at some point in the future, you will find joy and hope in your life again. As you will read in this book, your success will depend on how much hard work you're willing to put in. Use this book as your resource and come back to it often because it will speak to you differently each time you read it.*

*As you embark on this journey, know that I care. Know that you are not alone. There are millions of dads out there who have already traveled this path and survived.*

*We'll help you do the same.*

*Wishing you peace.*

*Kelly D. Farley*
*(630) 561-5989*
*Kelly@GrievingDads.com*
*GrievingDads.com*

# FOREWORD

Babies are supposed to grow up, aren't they? Long after they learn to crawl and the candles on their first birthday cakes are blown out, babies are supposed to grow up and say goodbye to their parents one day. Not the other way around.

But the reverse does happen. Way too often.

In fact, when it comes to babies who never get to grow up, the worst statistics suggest that up to twenty-five percent of the 4.4 million annual pregnancies in the United States result in the loss of the baby during pregnancy. Over one million of them are lost to miscarriage, 25,000 become victims of stillbirth, and still another 20,000 die before they even get to see a cake with one birthday candle on top.

All those babies who never got the chance to grow up leave behind an immeasurable amount of pain and grief that their parents must somehow absorb. The death of a baby is not something you ever get over. It's something you learn to live with. Unfortunately, it's not as easy as that sentence made it sound.

"Learning to live with it" has many levels. "It" is a pain that burrows all the way down and goes straight to the core of your being. It affects you in ways most people, including yourself, will never comprehend. It shakes your foundation in a way that makes you believe your world will crumble, and sometimes it does. It is a relentless enemy requiring an incredible amount of fortitude. It will likely be the greatest battle of your lifetime.

I know this because I have survived it twice over an eighteen-month period. The pain you experience will make you second-guess everything you see, touch, and feel. It will make you think you're going crazy at times, and it will force you to deal with all kinds of emotions. Some of these emotions will be more intense than you thought possible.

I've been there, and it was hard. My hope is that any grieving dad who reads this book is taking his first step toward realizing he never has to feel like he's alone. Since I wrote my first book, *Grieving Dads: To the Brink and Back*, I have heard from thousands of dads from around the world who have lost a child. Almost all of them carry the same sense of guilt, sadness, brokenness, and pain that society often overlooks.

I could not have known the impact my first book was going to have on those who read it. I began hearing from individual men and women, as well as various organizations from all over the world, telling me how much that book helped them. Some were seeking support for themselves, and others wanted to know how they could help the grieving men in their lives. It became obvious that *Grieving Dads: To the Brink and Back* was helping to fill a gap between the information meant to help grieving moms and the kind that didn't previously exist for grieving dads.

Another thing that became apparent to me since that book was published is that grieving dads who have lost a baby are an underserved group, grasping for something that will help them understand what has happened to them while offering hope that will pull them out of the despair and pain they are living with. The death of a baby reminds you in a harsh way that life isn't fair. In fact, it's downright ruthless at times. That's true for the moms who carried those babies in their wombs, but also for the fathers who carried them in their hearts. With those fathers in mind, the goal of this book is to shed light on the fact that it isn't just the mother who lost her baby. The father lost his baby too.

It seems like such a simple concept, but for far too long, the men who play a part in this terrible equation have been overlooked while the mother has been cared for. Fathers have often taken a back seat to the mom's needs in these awful situations. That is understandable and, in many ways, quite natural, because the mom carried the baby in her body. The resulting physical connection is undeniable. But as the dad, you too have lost your precious baby. You, too, deserve the compassion, recognition, and empathy clearly due to the mothers involved.

And certainly, you deserve a resource that can help you unravel everything you're feeling and all you're going through.

My hope is that this book becomes that resource.

CHAPTER 1

# NOT ALONE

QUESTIONS. WE ALL have them. Questions without answers, but we ask them anyway.

Questions like "Why me?" "How did this happen?" and "Don't bad things only happen to other people?" These are a few of the thousands of questions every grieving dad will ask to help him process what has happened. It's natural to ask questions.

When something bad—strike that—when something *devastating* happens in our lives, we instinctively ask these types of questions, whether we do it out loud or within the dark recesses of our minds.

Questions like "Why me?" are perfectly logical. But they have no logical answers. I wish I could answer that question for you, but I can't. I tried to answer it for myself, with zero success. I don't know why it happened to you and your baby, and I don't know why it happened to me and mine.

I would often ask the question, "Why me?" Why did this happen to me not only once, but twice? I've never found the answer to that question, and trust me, I've looked. But along my journey, I've learned I wasn't the only dad out there asking that specific question.

Not by a long shot.

Simply put, you are not alone with your questions. You may or may not take some small comfort in that fact, but many *millions* of fathers have, are, and will be going through the same things you're experiencing. That reality doesn't relieve the pain, but there could at least be some solace in the knowledge that you are not alone on this journey. At the very least, you can be sure the universe isn't singling you out or prescribing a fate completely unique to you. Not that you would wish this on anyone else, but knowing there are other men out there fighting the same fight does help a bit. At least it helped me.

Once I made room for the idea I wasn't the only guy on the planet who's been forced down this horrible path, I did find some small comfort. It helped me learn that bad things happen to people all the time; I was just lucky enough up until the moment I lost my children to be naive to that fact. I wish I still was that naive, but those are not the cards I have been dealt. And when you consider that literally millions of men have been dealt those very same cards, it does provide a bit of context and perspective even if it doesn't make you feel better about your own loss.

And what a loss it is.

Before experiencing this awful trauma, some dads had only their dreams of holding that approaching bundle of joy. Others had the pleasure of getting to do so—just to have their babies die shortly thereafter. All of us have held our babies in our hearts, determinedly trying to shield them from all forms of harm. Some of us never had the chance to meet our baby, but we still had the instinct to protect them.

Before any of this happened to me, I didn't know it existed. I didn't have any conscious awareness of people losing their babies. I didn't know how much the death of a baby affected the parents and everyone around them. My ignorance of these conditions was truly bliss.

In the early days after the death of my second child, Noah, as I was wrestling with my own survival, I began to write down some of my thoughts on paper. I thought if I wrote them down, I could capture what this pain feels like and others around me would understand what I was dealing with. The following is what I came up with:

> *"It's like being dropped deep into a body of water blindfolded at night. You are alone and in complete silence except for what you hear in your head. You don't know which way is up. The fear sets in, and you start to experience psychological and physical symptoms you may never have felt before. Fear turns to panic as you try to make sense of it all, grasping for help."*

There is no doubt that almost irreversible damage has affected your nervous system—or more accurately, trauma, as I've heard it described. Call it what you will, it doesn't change the way you feel inside.

Do my early thoughts shown above truly capture what it's like to lose a baby or what the aftermath of losing a baby might feel like? Not really, but it was the best I could do at the time. I encourage you to write your own description and share it with others around you. I'm not going to make any empty promises about such an approach being a cure-all. But I can tell you from direct experience that it helps. You, and the others you share it with, will at least know where your thoughts are at the time you write them down. I have often found it easier to write my thoughts down rather than say them out loud.

No matter how much I wrote or thought about losing my babies, it took a good long while before I began to accept certain realities. Concluding that there were no answers to any of my questions was tough but not the most difficult thing I had to do. That distinction goes to this lesson:

*"I couldn't go back to the guy I was before. That guy was gone."*

The harsh reality is that you will not be able to do that either. How could you go back to the guy you were before? The answer is you can't because after the loss of a baby, you know too much.

After such a crushing loss, you may no longer recognize the person in the mirror. You look vaguely familiar in physical features only. The look you see in your own eyes conveys so much pain, pain that no one on the street recognizes—and if they do, they sure as hell won't ask you about it. That would make *them* too uncomfortable.

I'm not going to sugarcoat this. Everything about it sucks.

What you are feeling is real. Let it be what it is. Stay with it, and by all means, resist the urge to give up.

Losing your baby is like having a brutal fight in some deep sludge, and there will be some days when you win the fight and some days when you lose. The trick is to get up the next day and start the fight all over again. To have any chance of winning more than just today's fight, it is essential that you process the loss you have experienced.

I mean, really process it. Deep down. You must go "there" to get "here."

This book will help you go "there" so that you can start building back the new you. It is imperative you acknowledge the loss of your baby for a multitude of reasons, but mostly because many around you will not.

Miscarriage, stillbirth, and even infertility issues are often dismissed with comments like, "You can try again" or "You can always adopt."

But no matter the comments, we will certainly mourn "what should have been." So many memories to be made and so many life experiences to be enjoyed with our children—the prospect of it all brought great anticipation and an incredible sense of wonder and love.

And all those things were taken away. Brutally, without warning, and without an ounce of mercy.

With all that in mind, I encourage you to stick with this book until the end. It will be tough at times, so know that going in. There is a part of you that already knows that; I mean, what could possibly be more "tough" than losing your baby? Realizing that fact is one thing. Facing it is quite a different matter.

Truly looking your loss right in the face is what this book is all about. I am here to tell you, from direct personal experience and from what I've learned from the thousands of other dads I've met, that if you're going to have any chance at life after the loss of your baby, you must dig deep and connect with others. You must learn to be transparent.

You must surrender to some emotions you have undoubtedly been conditioned to think you were supposed to bury with your baby.

Above all, you must remember that you are not alone and that you must not let fear of judgment or fear of socially engraved thoughts we have as men stop you from healing.

If you can open your mind for a moment and embrace these ideas, then healing is exactly what you will start to do.

CHAPTER 2

# FULL IMPACT

IT'S BEEN EIGHTEEN years since I lost Katie and sixteen years since I lost Noah. I still have days where I feel the impact of their loss.

The loss of one baby to miscarriage and another to stillbirth is something that resurfaces from time to time, despite what many might think would be an "adequate" amount of time to grieve.

I have learned to navigate life despite this damage—but make no mistake, it's still right here in front of me. It will be right there in front of you, too.

No matter how you got to this point, I know it has made a full, head-on impact on everything and everyone in your life. This full impact is unavoidable, and it happens whether they couldn't find a heartbeat at your "routine" checkup, you watched your baby die during delivery, you found your baby not breathing in their crib, or you had to make a life-or-death decision on their behalf.

At first, the impact of such a loss manifests in uncontrollable horror and despair.

Suffice it to say your emotions will race from shock and denial at the beginning to guilt, self-blame, and hopelessness at various points along the road.

Raw instinct pushes us toward trying to survive these kinds of emotions. However, over time, you will learn you don't have to point your compass toward mere survival. Instead, you can learn to thrive. This is a lesson I have finally absorbed, but it didn't happen without a whole lot of patience and a complete overhaul of my perspectives. For example, like most men, once I got past the denial and anger stages of grief, I began to think of my losses as problems that needed to be solved.

But let me be clear:

*The loss of a baby is NOT something you can solve! It is something you must* process.

Grasping that simple concept involves completely remaking the way we, as men, are wired to think. In general, men often see the obstacles in their lives as everyday problems that need everyday solutions. The more difficult hurdles we face in life need more creative solutions, right?

Not really—at least not when it comes to the loss of your baby.

Simply put, losing a baby results in pure, unrestrained trauma. And although this trauma doesn't present itself physically, the damage is still there, and that's the part that is challenging for you and others to understand. It's much easier to see and accept the physical damage blunt force trauma causes. The psychological impact is much more difficult to detect and comprehend. But make no mistake, it's there and it needs to be addressed.

However, before we can address it, we need to understand what it is and what it looks like. During my mission to understand my pain, I decided to research emotional trauma and the symptoms it causes. I came across several articles that helped explain "emotional and psychological trauma" and the impact they can have on a person.

It was enlightening.

All the symptoms I had experienced—a few of which I still deal with—were right there in front of me in bold, black letters.

Here are a few of the more prominent symptoms you may currently have or could possibly experience in the future:

- Shock, denial, or disbelief
- Anger, irritability, mood swings
- Guilt, shame, self-blame.
- Sad or hopeless feelings
- Insomnia and nightmares
- Confusion, and difficulty concentrating
- Anxiety and fear
- Withdrawing from others.
- Disconnected or numb feelings
- Fatigue

It took me several years and the right doctor to understand that what I experienced was trauma. I was diagnosed with posttraumatic stress disorder (PTSD) and treated accordingly.

It's important for you to understand that this isn't just grief. What you and I experienced is the true definition of trauma:

*"a deeply distressing or disturbing experience."*

This trauma is the death of your baby. If this isn't a deeply distressing or disturbing experience, I don't know what is. Don't let anyone tell you otherwise.

I share this message with others in my writings and workshops. I am never surprised to hear from other dads who describe similar experiences.

One of them, Tony, described his response to the trauma he was experiencing the same way I would have at that stage of my journey. Namely, he began to find it difficult to remain motivated at his job. Tasks and relationships at work that had been rewarding in the past now seemed "trivial and meaningless."

My reply to Tony was essentially, "I hear you, brother." I found it—strike that—I still find it challenging to care about things at work like deadlines, timesheets, policies, procedures, meetings—the list keeps going.

In the grand scheme of life, these things do not matter to me anymore. Even years later.

Some would say I have a bad attitude.

I would say, "I have a new perspective about what is and isn't important in life."

The people who say I have a bad attitude are the same people who have been fortunate enough to not say goodbye to a baby.

Those who have had to say goodbye understand my "bad attitude."

This is important to remember when you get frustrated with yourself because you feel like you are not the "old you." You feel that way because you are indeed not the old you. Rather, you have experienced a full-impact injury that is hard to see and comprehend. Call it PTSD (my own doctor called it exactly that) or whatever else, but there was damage done to you because of losing your baby.

Even now, years after experiencing this trauma, I sometimes tend to judge myself for not being the guy I was before the loss of my first baby. When I look back at that time in my life, I realize I have come a long way from those dark days, and I recognize it's OK to enjoy life and relax whenever I can. It took a long time to come to that realization, but I now allow myself to feel happiness and peace in my life.

Those two things are not always so easy to come by even if you haven't lost a baby. But if you learn to surrender to the grief process and acknowledge the trauma—if you allow it to run its course instead of fighting it—one day you will come to realize there is hope, and there are brighter days ahead. I promise you the loss of your baby is not a puzzle you can unscramble or a code you can crack.

If you want to see those brighter days, you must learn to *process* your grief instead of trying to fight it.

More on that later. For now, let's move on to some of the other things you're going to have to recognize if you are committed to making life worth living again.

CHAPTER 3

# DEFINED ROLES—A MYTH

ASK ANY FATHER what he thinks his primary purpose is here on earth, and you're likely to get the same answer: to provide for his family, and more important, to *protect* his family.

Especially his children, right?

So, when we lose a baby to an untimely death, it's natural for us to feel like we failed to protect our family.

I know I did. I suspect you are feeling that way, too.

After all, if given the choice, we would fall on the sword and change places with our baby—and we would do it without a moment's hesitation or forethought.

If only it were our choice to make, right?

Well, it is not. If it were, this whole "loss of a baby" thing would go away because there's not a father alive who wouldn't rather be dead if it meant his baby would have the chance to live on.

Men are the strong ones, right?

Our "role" is to protect and be the pillar of strength for our family.

Society has shaped the role of the father in the family dynamic to be pretty much the same across all cultures and walks of life. That shape has taken the same basic form over thousands of years, and despite some desire to define all humans as "equal in all aspects," certain elements of the man's place in society remain largely unchanged. That doesn't mean it's right; it's just the way it is, for now.

A shift away from these defined roles will not occur overnight. But that doesn't mean *you* have to live that role or accept someone else's definition of "strength."

From the time we're able to understand the most rudimentary communication, we men are subjected to society's ideas about what it means to be a man. For many of us, the concept of being "strong" and "manly" is programmed into our heads at the earliest stages of our lives. From "girls play with dolls, boys play with cars" to "rub some dirt on it and get back in the game," young boys are trained to be what civilization thinks they ought to be. And what we "ought to be" can best be described as emotionless, tough creatures who wouldn't dare show a shred of weakness, ever.

Indeed, even the most committed equalists are prone to

look at men as sturdy, robust physical beings who should be called upon when something heavy needs to be carried.

And it would be hard to think of something heavier than the loss of a baby, right?

Right.

Losing your baby is a crushing experience; the pain burrows in, and it throbs like a rumbling herd of angry bulls. Those bulls come straight at you, and there's no chance to get out of the way. That's fine because as men who have been living society's lies about what we should be, we run with the bulls, and in the process, we come to feel just as angry as they are.

Men are allowed to be angry, right? That's what we do. We get angry. But if we cry, that gets weird for everyone.

Why is that?

Why does society say it's OK for us to be angry, but crying over heartbreak is not acceptable?

Anger is the one emotion society finds perfectly acceptable for men to show. Hell, there are even times when we are *encouraged* to get mad. Ever hear a sports fan say he wished his team's coach would get fired up at the refs? Or a spouse urging their husband to adopt a stern tone (*Just wait until your father gets home!*) to scold their child?

There are a multitude of emotions that set in after the death of a child, and I have experienced all of them. But the one that stands out to me is anger. The word alone provokes many thoughts and images. Like most men, I saw anger as the singular emotion society allowed me to have without too much judgment.

Unfortunately, many grieving dads get stuck at anger and never move past it because society is uncomfortable with a grown man openly expressing his sadness. As a result, the anger a grieving dad feels begins to boil over and manifests itself as physical and psychological issues.

I have heard from thousands of grieving dads over the last several years, and many have shared with me some of the things that angered them:

- They become angry at themselves for not being able to protect their child.
- They become angry because the life they once knew is gone.
- They become angry at God for allowing the loss to occur.
- They become angry because the world keeps moving after their loss, like nothing happened.
- They are angry at people who may have had a role in the death of their child.
- They are angry because some people around them want them to "get over it and move on."
- They are angry because they lost control of themselves and their emotions.
- They are angry at their employers for not understanding that their performance at work has been forever affected and that they are not the same person they were before.
- They are angry because they have lost hope and can't seem to get it back.

Any of these sound familiar? I'll bet at least some do. All of them are understandable, and all of them are natural—even if you think they shouldn't be.

If men were "allowed" to show emotions that looked less like anger and more like sorrow, maybe we could move toward surviving the loss of a baby more effectively.

But we're not allowed to, right?

Wrong!

Absolutely, positively wrong! Forget what society has taught you about what it means to be a man. Take a moment to consider a simple alternative instead:

*What if the only person you need "permission" from is you?*

If you can accept that concept, even for a moment, then maybe you are "allowed" to be something other than angry after all.

It took me a long time to come to that conclusion—but once I did, once I gave myself permission to acknowledge the impossibly profound sadness I was feeling after the loss of my babies, I finally took the first step toward recovering from the serious damage the sadness was causing me and others.

And let me tell you, once I let go of the anger and surrendered to the despair, the way I cried couldn't be described as crying at all. It was more like hysterical sobbing, and it was thoroughly unrestrained and equally unapologetic. The pent-up pain came from a place so deep it made a sound as it was released. That cleansing howl and those tears rinsed the anger away and made me realize that crying wasn't a symbol of weakness in any way, shape, or form.

It's therapeutic to cry; it's our body's way of protecting itself. We were not designed to carry this amount of pain, yet we still try to do it out of fear of being perceived as weak.

If you're not going to cry about *this*, what in the world will you ever cry about?

It took me a long time to get comfortable crying in front of someone else. It took years and I fought like hell to hold it in, but I became worn out from fending it off. It would have been much easier to let go of that "defined role" and accept the fact that I was heartbroken over the loss of my babies.

I have no doubt I inflicted a lot of mental damage on myself as a result of buying into others' expectations of how I was supposed to handle my pain. I don't want that for you.

Even though I became comfortable with my own emotions, it still took me a while to get used to sitting with other grieving dads while they fought back tears when telling me their stories. Years of programming don't go away overnight. I can honestly say it no longer bothers me, and I find it a true honor to be able to sit with other grieving dads while they share their stories and emotional pain.

For me, that first big cry opened the door to a hallway that led away from the brink of destruction. If the hallway had been lined with pictures, they'd be visual representations of every emotion a man will feel along the path of grieving.

And yes, every now and again a picture of the old anger would pop up somewhere along the walls, but it seemed to be painted a bit differently after I began to let other feelings in.

At least this was a more manageable hell. And realistically, "managing" what we are going through is about the best we can hope for during the grieving process.

Because no matter what anyone tells you, there is no way to "get over" the loss of your baby. Coming from this horrible experience myself, I am here to tell you you'll never get over it—but I promise you can live with it.

You have to give yourself permission.

CHAPTER 4

# PEOPLE—WHAT TO EXPECT

"THERE ARE NO words."

Everyone has heard that saying, and we all know it to be true when it comes to communicating with someone who has lost a loved one. There are no words. *Nothing* we could say to someone who has lost their baby is going to console them or lessen the damage.

Everyone knows that, but it doesn't stop them from trying. Often, that comes with bad results.

Know that moving forward.

People are going to do and say things that will shock you. I could write a book specifically on this topic. I have heard examples of these shocking experiences from most of the grieving dads I've met over the years.

It's true that most people have no idea how to handle interacting with someone who has experienced such profound loss. But I must ask, when faced with an impossible task, why do some people insist on making a spectacular mess of the attempt?

Simply put, this is a paralyzing loss most people never have to endure. They don't know what it's like to lose a baby. They are going to say things and do things that hurt you or piss you off. It's not necessarily intentional; they just don't know what you're dealing with.

People in your life will not understand what you are going through because they never had to travel this path. There will be family members, coworkers, and friends who will pull away because they don't know how to handle you. They will give you space, being careful to avoid "bringing up the subject" because they think it will be too hard for you. In reality, most are not sure how to address this terrible subject, or at a minimum, they are too uncomfortable with such a taboo topic.

Some people, maybe the smarter ones, will disappear for a while to give you space. Some will test the waters and reappear later to see if you are "back to the old you." Some will never return until you reach out to them, if you ever decide to do so. If not, that's OK, too.

Some people around you, specifically those who are trying to have a baby or are currently pregnant, will avoid you because they think you might be contagious.

They don't want to catch what you caught. If they don't think about what happened to you or your baby, they think it won't happen to them. Seems logical, right?

Of course not, but that is how some people think. They can't bear the thought of it happening to them, so they don't think about it and try to avoid the subject (and you) like the plague.

When someone in your life finally musters the courage to make conversation at all, it often starts with something like, "How is your wife doing?" This is purely a result of society's built-in predisposition to assume the loss of a baby is almost exclusively a problem for the mom—not the dad.

This is a universal experience among the grieving dads I have met and interviewed. We've all experienced it at one time or another.

You will hear platitudes like "Things happen for a reason" and "God doesn't give you more than you can handle." All well-intended, but they don't help. Not even a little. In fact, these types of comments can cause more harm than good. But you must learn to let them bounce off you and forgive the messenger. They are trying to help. Fortunately for them, they have no idea of the pain you carry.

These kinds of things are bad enough, but I must warn you: you need to prepare yourself for worse. If you are like many of the grieving dads I've met, you are going to get calls, emails, and junk mail from companies wanting to sell you the things you expected to buy for your new baby:

*Doesn't the new, happy family need some organic baby formula? How about the softest diapers on the planet? Sure, they cost a little more, but isn't your baby worth it?*

These companies get ahold of marketing lists indicating that you and your partner were expecting a baby. But apparently, no one ever updates the list to let them know your baby died. Be ready for these calls or emails. They can be major triggers, and it doesn't help that the marketer on the other end isn't at fault. You're likely to blame them anyway.

The angst doesn't stop there. Next up is your situation at work. Your boss will likely expect you to be back at it quickly because, damn it, we need productivity and billable time! We need your head in the game!

There's a problem with all that. Your head isn't in the game at all. It's in a fog. A deep, dark fog as thick as the despair you are feeling after this terrible loss.

There's more. What has happened to you and your baby will affect everyone in your circle. Your friends and their "problems" will seem irrelevant, and soon they will notice that's exactly how you feel.

Your extended family (parents, grandparents, siblings) will feel powerless to help you, and they will have no idea how to go about it, anyway.

Your spouse will be in as much anguish as you are and trying their best to hold their shit together.

And last, if you have other (living) children, they will

feel forgotten—or at least less important—even as they deal with the loss of their brother or sister.

So, between the pressures at home to be the man of the house and the pressures at work to be a productive contributor, the burdens become overwhelming in short order. And all the while, your personal grieving is something you'll be expected to do on your "own" time.

When all this is going on, you'll be asking yourself, "How can the world keep moving? My baby has died!" Yet the world does keep moving. All you want is for the planet to stop for a moment and acknowledge that your baby has died, to give them the respect they deserve.

Instead, people still go about their lives as if nothing has happened.

In their worlds, it hasn't. They all keep moving through life, absorbed by the "worries" associated with their careers, their personal finances, their next vacations, or what's on the menu for tonight's dinner.

You, meanwhile, will be slowly dying on the inside. You are consumed with one thing and one thing only: the death of your child. Nothing else will seem to matter—nothing at all. For a while, that's OK.

I've learned that for the most part, people have good intentions. They want to help you, but they don't know how. They will say things like "Let me know if there is anything I can do or if you need anything."

You'll want to reply with "How about bringing my baby back?" But as you know, that isn't possible. What I encourage you to do is to tell them what you need. You may not know the answer to that question early on, but over time, you will.

Take my advice on this matter, as one who has been through all of this. Allow yourself the authority to decide whether the people who have said or done something to you deserve forgiveness—or not. I wouldn't suggest punishing them by making them feel worse than they already do, but I wholeheartedly endorse whatever *internal* response seems appropriate.

Dealing with close family or friends may be the one exception to the "Let it all out" rule that I support in general. I'm not saying hold it all back; even close loved ones need to be enlightened from time to time.

All I'm saying is that you should try to practice restraint if you hope to have a future relationship with these people. Your emotions are running hot. Remember the anger thing we discussed earlier? Sometimes, we will bite back hard when we feel like others have intentionally hurt us. Most of the time, the hurt they cause is not intentional.

At the same time, if it's clear it was intentional, feel free to let them have it.

Some people (friends, family, and strangers) are going to say and do all the right things. Keep those people close.

Other people are going to say or do stupid things too often. But it's up to you to decide which of them deserve the benefit of the doubt and which don't.

CHAPTER 5

# TURNING POINT

IF YOU'RE ANYTHING like me, at some point during your grief journey, you're going to hit a wall.

There will come a day when you must have some difficult discussions with yourself because what you've been doing isn't working. Regardless of whether you recently lost your child or if you've been fighting the loss for a while, you are likely experiencing some or all the following:

- Increased isolation
- Depression/despair
- Loss of hope—no light at the end of the tunnel
- Panic attacks
- Loss of the desire to live—you're at a point where it doesn't matter if you live or die

- Suicidal thoughts
- Self-medicating—alcohol/drugs
- Barely hanging on

The discussion with yourself starts with a simple question:

*"Do you want to survive this and get back to a semi-normal life?*

If so, you must prepare yourself to do the necessary hard work. You will have to make a firm, conscious choice to fight on.

Put another way, you must desperately want to be happy again and be willing to do what it takes to get there. In fact, you must recognize that happiness itself is a choice. It's a choice you decide to make, multiple times a day.

Or not.

And beyond all that, you also must decide that it's OK to *want* to be happy again.

Like most grieving dads, you are likely to navigate your path in your own way for a while. But if it's not working and the choice to become happy again seems impossible to make, you must change your approach.

It took me three years of fighting it to finally realize I needed to change my approach. I can honestly say if I hadn't, I am not sure I would be here today. I'm not sure I would have survived. I was dying slowly, and I knew it.

My day of reckoning came during a cold, gray Midwest December. I had called in sick to work because I was not doing well mentally. It was about seven months after our second loss, and I was still trying to do things my way—which meant fighting through the loss alone.

That morning, I was having panic attacks and was literally on my hands and knees in my living room, begging for relief. It was at that moment I realized there was no way I could beat this by myself.

I needed help.

And I thought maybe, just maybe, some of the advice my primary care doctor was giving me was good. He advised me to seek counseling and consider an antidepressant.

I originally said "no" to both, but as I was kneeling on that floor, it became abundantly clear that this was not a fight I could win on my own.

For sure, I needed help in a big way.

To this day, I can't help but wonder how much damage I caused myself because of my own sense of pride. The healing process could have started two years earlier if I had known or accepted the secret to surviving this and everything else in life.

The secret is,

***"Surrender to the process."***

OK, it's not a secret; it's more of a directive. But what does it mean?

It means you must lower your guard and set aside your pride and your ego. You must ask for help and be open to the concept. You must become transparent with your story and your emotions. You must put all your cards on the table. You must allow yourself to become vulnerable.

The "I got this" attitude must be abandoned and replaced with an "I need help!" attitude.

You don't have this. It has you.

And the sooner you recognize that, the sooner you can get around to choosing happiness again.

With that in mind, let's discuss the process of surrendering and what it might look like.

You will hear me talk about transparency and vulnerability a few times in this book. That's not by accident. I want you to understand the importance of embracing this concept.

How do you become transparent and vulnerable? With a lot of hard work. And you're going to have to get comfortable with being uncomfortable.

You must find ways to tell your story and your baby's story. And I mean *everything* about the story. Even the dark and heartbreaking stuff.

Did you watch your baby take their last breath?

Did you deliver a baby that was already dead?

Did the fertility treatments your wife went through end with a miscarriage?

Did you have to make the heartbreaking decision to terminate the pregnancy because of severe fetal anomalies or to remove your baby from life support?

What is your story?

Stop saying, "It's too hard to go there." I know it's hard; I've had to go back and relive my story hundreds, if not thousands, of times.

But the more you tell your story, the more your story becomes just another story in your life. It's a difficult story, but it's still a story that must be told repeatedly until it no longer hurts so badly to "go there."

You can get these stories out in a lot of different ways. Here are a few that I have found helpful:

- Discuss your story with your partner.
- Work with a counselor or a grief coach.
- Find a group of other grieving dads.
- Seek support groups (in-person and/or virtually).
- Find a mentor—someone who went through the experience a few years ago and has already done the hard work.
- Go to workshops on the topic.
- Write letters to your child.
- Journal/write a personal book about your journey—you don't have to share it.
- Pray.

Once you start telling your story, the emotions are finally going to be released. You don't need to apologize for them or fight them; just let them be what they are.

Bottom line: you must become transparent and vulnerable.

Yeah, I know, I wasn't particularly good at being vulnerable either. But as with anything, the more you practice, the better you become at it. I'm still not perfect at being vulnerable by any means, but I've come a long way. I have no doubt you can do the same.

So, as you move through the day-to-day slog in the aftermath of your loss, it's inevitable that the day will come where you finally hit the wall. At that point, you are at a crossroads.

You either stay on your path, or you make the decision to change course. Call this a turning point, if you will.

It takes a lot of courage to make these changes or adjust how you would normally respond to adversity. But keep this in mind: unless you have already experienced the loss of a baby, *this is like no adversity you have ever faced before!*

It is relentless despair that will take you places you cannot even begin to comprehend until you are there.

None of us wants to be on this path.

I certainly wish I never had to travel it, but that is the hand we've been dealt, so we must dig deep and find the courage to do these things:

- Get out of bed today. You are going to have days where you don't want to get out of bed and face another day without your baby, but you must. I get it: you don't want to go out of the house and try to blend back into society. The world as you know it has forever been changed, and it's scary. But the path toward a more normal life must start somewhere, and getting out of bed is mission critical in that regard.

- Show your tears and all your other emotions. We all know that "big boys don't cry," right? I mean this is what we are taught as young boys, to be "strong." But one thing they forgot to tell us is that strength doesn't require stifling our emotions. In fact, it takes a lot more strength to have the courage to cry! There is a time and place to be "strong," but the loss of a child is not one of those times. You must throw away old ideas and allow yourself to be open to new beliefs and coping skills. You must accept the fact that some of your beliefs might be wrong—or, as in this case, outdated. You held those beliefs before you could even fathom the loss of your baby, let alone live through it. Now that you are living it, it's time to recognize the rules have changed.

- Face your fears. Some fears will go away while others will remain. The fear of losing someone else in your life, such as another child or a spouse, is a common one. It never goes away, quite frankly. Others do. For example, the fear of losing your job or the fear of taking risks in life and business seems to be less worrisome after the loss of your baby. There's a little bit of freedom that comes with that. The freedom of not caring what others think. You are going to live life your way and on your terms, because you know what they don't know, and that is the pain of losing a child. That pain is hard to replicate—unless, of course, you lose another child. No matter what anybody says or does to you, it could never be as bad as the day you had to say goodbye to your baby. That day will forever be the worst day of your life. The loss of a job, in comparison, is just that. It's just a job.

- Accept support. Look, we can't do this alone. We need the help and comfort of others to truly process this loss. It's OK to accept help; we all need it from time to time. I always prided myself on the "doing it on my own" mantra. I didn't need or ask for help from anyone else. I was in control of my life and my emotions. Until I wasn't. I wasn't in a good place at all, and as hard as I tried, I couldn't pull it together. It took me a while to realize this was a fight I couldn't handle on my own. I needed others to pull me through the sludge of grief. Once I accepted help, the heavy burden I had been carrying got lighter and lighter over time.

- Reach out to others who are also on this path. It helps to have someone you can lean on when you are having a rough day, and vice versa. After experiencing the loss of my second child, I knew I couldn't survive it on my own. I needed to be around others who were on this journey because they "got it." There is an old adage that says, "Misery loves company." However, I believe whoever wrote that had it slightly wrong. I personally would tweak it to read, "Misery *needs* company." There is no reason you must go through this alone. Find your community, and you will become a part of a brotherhood of other grieving dads who will have your back.

- Walk into a room full of strangers at a support group. This might be the last thing on earth you want to do, but it's a crucial part of the vulnerability I mentioned earlier. You will find yourself trying to hold your own emotions together, and all you will see is the pain on the faces of the others in the room. But take it one step further—don't just show up and not say anything. Open up. Share your story and experiences as well. You are likely to break down emotionally, but becoming emotional around others who have lost a child is a natural response—and it's precisely the one everybody in the room is expecting. And that is the critical difference! Up to this point, you may have tried unloading on friends and family—but if they haven't experienced the loss of a child, they cannot possibly understand the way people in these support groups do.

- Keep going to those support groups because the strangers in that room will not be strangers for long. A community of mutual support will develop, and you will connect with others. Maybe you will not connect with everyone, but you will form a bond with some people on this journey. If you stick with it, you too will be the stranger in the room when a new grieving parent finds the courage to show up.

- Give support. I have had many "turning points" along my journey, but the one that brought me full circle was my conscious decision to help others through this nightmare. I realized early on there wasn't much support material for grieving dads, so I made a promise to myself that I would create something that could be helpful. I wasn't sure what that something was going to look like, but it gave me a purpose and some much needed hope at a period in my life when I had none. At the time, I was at a point where I had to rebuild my life because everything I thought I knew and everything I thought I was had disappeared in an instant. I had to face the harsh reality that I couldn't go back to the old me. I had to find my new "why." I never would have guessed that decision would change the course of my life as much as it did. Not only did it give me hope, but it also gave me a mission. A mission to reach back and pull others out of the sludge and onto this path of recovery. As a result, I have had the privilege of sitting with other grieving dads when they told their stories for the first time. And I've listened to many dads who called me late at night not knowing what they were going to say except that they needed to talk to someone.

It's a true gift to be able to reach out and put your hand on another dad's shoulder or offer him encouragement when he wipes away his tears. Most of us men get uncomfortable when other men around us become emotionally distraught.

I was no different, but my thoughts on this subject have changed because of how other people, mostly complete strangers, reached out to me and offered me compassion. They didn't have to, but I am extremely grateful they did.

Once you are the recipient of such compassion, you understand the power of a touch or of someone who has the patience to sit and listen. I encourage you to offer those same gifts to others once you have the strength.

The network you build will be your safety net on the days you can't seem to function. They will help you, and you will help them on the days they are down and you are up. It can work both ways and I promise you, once you embrace these ideas, you will be on the way to your own turning point in this difficult journey.

You will be on your way to turning a corner that has some real hope and promise on the other side.

CHAPTER 6

# GET BACK UP

YOU ARE BRUISED and broken. You have taken a blow that has knocked you to the ground. But you know you cannot stay there.

Do not give up. Get up!

You must get back up and fight! Every day.

No one expects you to win every fight. That is unrealistic. But you will have to fight every fight.

Are you going to be the guy who lets the death of your baby define you or *redefine* you?

It's your decision either way. One decision keeps you sad, and you become known as the guy who can't seem to function in society again.

However, the other one—redefining yourself—allows you to find new hope and peace in your life.

If you are determined to get back up, the first thing you must do is empty yourself. It is imperative to empty everything bad you remember, have experienced, have felt, and have witnessed. It's a heavy load that you must empty because if it's left to fester, its poison will overwhelm you.

There are going to be days you don't think this "emptying yourself" thing is working. This process is so slow that you won't even realize you are making progress. But you are.

My own "emptying" started not long after I made the decision to seek help. I went to a male counselor the hospital referred me to, and I sat there for an hour and poured my guts out to this guy, tears, snot, and all. When I finally shut up, he said to me, "If I wasn't sitting here right now listening to you and seeing you in person, I would have thought you were a woman telling me her story."

That surprised me, and I asked him what he meant.

He could tell he had made me angry.

He said, "It's not often that I have a guy in my office willing to be so vulnerable and express so much pain." I never went back to him because he was over an hour away from where I lived, but his comment, although it seemed insulting at the time, opened my mind to the notion of "letting it all out."

In addition to this epiphany, this counselor gave me one of the best tools to track my progress. During our discussion, I had told him that I didn't feel like I was getting any better even though I believed I was doing all the hard work of emptying myself. He assured me that I had probably already experienced some progress, but because it was such a slow change, I didn't recognize it.

The counselor told me to track my progress so that I could see it gradually over time. I took his advice and created a spreadsheet that I would fill out twice a day—once in the morning and once in the evening. I would assign a score from one to ten, with ten being the highest. I would rank my mood, appetite, sleep, energy, and overall feeling on this scale of one to ten. I did this for a year.

On the days I didn't feel like I was making progress, I would go to this spreadsheet and look back to see if there were any improvements in my rankings. Using this tool, I could see that my rankings in every category eventually went up over time. There would be days where I would score a two but a few weeks later, I would notice that I had gone up to a five. Like I said, it's a slow process, but the key is to remain calm, to trust the process, and to not panic. It is three steps forward and two-and-a-half steps back. But it does get easier with time if you do the hard work.

If you don't, I'm not sure it ever gets easier. I hate to think where I would be today if I did not surrender.

I wish I had better news for you, but getting up off the floor and emptying yourself takes a lot of time. I decided, regardless of how long it was going to take, that my life was at stake and I wasn't going to give up. I don't want you to, either. There is light at the end of that long dark tunnel, but it's ever so faint; you might not even see it, early on.

One of the guys who had trouble seeing in such dim light was John, a dad who read my first book and wanted to tell me his story. He called and told me that he had been fighting the death of his two-month-old baby for three years and had never told his story to anyone. I asked him how that approach was working out for him, and he responded, "Not good. I've been drinking a lot more and having a difficult time functioning." He was having a difficult time getting back up because he didn't do the hard work of surrendering as discussed in the previous chapter. He was trying to circumvent the process by taking a shortcut.

There are no shortcuts.

If you are going to fight, you need to go into battle healthy—not with one hand tied behind your back and with little hope of success. Instead, you must run toward your pain and face it head on.

You must lean into it if you have any hope of getting back up and living a life where you don't just survive—you thrive.

Part of going into battle "healthy" involves recognizing that many of your core beliefs are wrong. For example, the idea that bad things only happen to other people is one of the principles we believe—right up until tragedy strikes us in a personal way. After the loss of your baby, you become very much aware that you are part of that "other people" group, and once you accept that, you need to examine other long-held convictions, too.

Take the conviction that you are who you are, and you'll never change.

Let me tell you, the death of a baby changes all aspects

of who you once were. Some of those changes are for the better, and some are for the worse.

In my own case, those changes made me start to look at life differently. I started to take it all in. I decided to live life as simply as possible (believe me, I'm still working on that). I don't rush through my day anymore. Work is not my priority. Making money is not my priority. Chasing material possessions is not my priority.

Instead, my priorities are taking in the moment; my relationship with my wife; my friendship with my dog; helping others when I can; and, for sure, my overall health. I still have moments of sadness; they will always be there, but I know they will not last forever.

A few weeks back, I was in the car with a couple of coworkers, and I made a comment about all the wildflowers that were growing in the fields on both sides of the road. I asked them if they ever take the time to notice them. One of the guys said, "I never notice them, but I notice that you do." I smiled and thought to myself how much I loved the fact that others notice the new me. I truly do take time to "smell the roses." I see the beauty and innocence in animals I never saw before. I see pain in others I never used to pay attention to. As a result, I feel a sense of peace I haven't had since I was a child.

In short, I've learned through my experiences that the most valuable thing isn't money. It is peace of mind and time.

Time to live life on your terms.

Remarkably, not everything that changes after the

death of a baby is bad. One of those things is that at the very least, we know we've already experienced the worst day of our lives.

After you go through something as profound as the death of a baby, you realize you will never encounter anything worse. Quite frankly, you begin to not care what others think or say. There is nothing anyone can possibly do or say that could ever be more damaging than the death of your baby.

Today, when I see people at work running around trying to hit deadlines and stressing out like it's the worst possible thing they must deal with, I laugh inside. I don't let work get to me like I used to. I still do my job, but I don't stress out about letting my boss down or anything along those lines.

What's the worst thing that could happen? I might get fired?

Let's see. Get fired or lose a baby? Which is worse?

I think I'll go with the loss of a baby.

People who haven't experienced this merciless loss cannot possibly understand what real worries are about. Earlier in my journey through grief, I'd get upset when people would say, "I am having the worst day of my life; I got a flat tire on the way to work!" or something along those lines.

Now I laugh to myself and think, "You have no idea what a bad day is." Lucky for them.

I found that this way of thinking is liberating because you are not out to impress anyone. When you don't care, it removes the stress of trying to impress others or to live life by their rules and expectations. It creates a sense of mental freedom from things that don't matter in the big picture of life.

This new change in perspective (some would call it a bad attitude, but it's not; it's an adjustment to how I see things) has made me better at my job. It's also made me more honest than I used to be. I have always spoken my mind, but I tend to do it more often and more bluntly.

I see so many people around me afraid of confrontation or of having a difficult conversation, but those things don't bother me anymore. It's like that filter has been removed. I don't look for confrontation, but I do prefer honest discussions. I call people out on their bullshit (and expect others to do the same to me), or I challenge them if I disagree with what they're saying. I am not trying to be an ass to others—in fact, I interact with them in a calm and professional way. But I refuse to take shit from anyone else, regardless of who they are or what their title is.

The old me was a mentally and emotionally strong guy who could weather any storm that came his way. After the deaths of Katie and Noah and in the aftermath of trying to survive, I realized the "old me" looked at life from a narrow perspective and that I was caught up in the rat race of life, living for my own shallow wants.

While dragging myself through all the pain, I learned that even after you experience such a profound life event, you can pick up the pieces and put them back together again. Those pieces will never fit in quite the same way as they did before your life was shattered, but I learned to make them fit just the same.

Although it is not possible to go back to the man you used to be, I believe you can become a wiser, stronger, and more compassionate person who has a better understanding of life.

I've learned that life certainly has a way of teaching you how to live it.

CHAPTER 7

# LEGACY

WHAT IS YOUR "why"?

What is going to give you the energy to live again? To help you overcome the despair and find the hope you will undoubtedly experience at some point along this journey? What is the one thing that is going to get you out of bed every day and help you rebuild the new you?

I know, it's a great question and one I still ask myself because the answer is ever changing and evolving, like life. I'm not the same person I was before I lost Katie and Noah, and I am not the same person I was in the years following their loss. However, I have learned to adapt and pursue things that give me joy, hope, and peace, and most important, I have learned to honor my children. I have taken it upon myself to try to live a life that would make them proud of their dad. I found that to be one of the secrets. I've learned that I could pull myself out of the despair I was experiencing by taking my *pain* and turning it into my *purpose.*

I wish I could give you the answer to your own question of "what is my why," but I can't. The "why" is different for everyone. It's personal because we all experience something different.

Some of you already have children while some of you do not. Some of you went through fertility treatments but may never have your own children. And some of you have suffered multiple losses. Our "why" cannot help but be different; I've spoken to dads in all kinds of situations, with all kinds of "whys."

Some of those dads created nonprofits in their children's honor. Some realized they couldn't have children, so they walked away from successful (yet unfulfilling) careers to do something more meaningful. Others decided to be counselors so that they could help people deal with such a tragic loss.

Whatever you choose, it doesn't have to be for a lifetime. Your "why" could end up being the right one even for a single season in your life. The profound and overwhelming loss you have experienced can create something powerful and meaningful, or if you let it, it can create brokenness and rage. I, and many of the other dads I've met, have experienced creating both—and I can tell you, working toward a life of meaning to honor your child is by far the better choice.

You must find *your* purpose, not mine, not someone else's. Yours. It's a difficult thing to do, especially while you are walking around with a broken heart. It's hard to find clarity when you are in this fog of despair, but you must keep searching for it. It takes time to find, but when you do, go all in.

I want to be clear that legacy work doesn't have to be focused only on your children, but they can be the fuel you need to get started. Maybe you didn't have the guts to make it happen before, and you let fear guide you rather than your instincts. Either way, if the loss of a child doesn't give you the guts to alter your approach to life, nothing probably will.

The loss of my children pushed a reset button for me. I knew I couldn't go back to the guy I was before. I tried, because it was all I knew and it was comfortable—or at the very least it was familiar. Although at the time, I wasn't all that inspired in my daily life, I found the concept of being the "old" me to be reassuring and easy. But before long, I realized there was no going back. That part of my life was over. I knew I was going to have to shove "easy" aside and get *uncomfortable* with making changes in my life. This was not a happy realization; at the time it seemed like a big negative because I didn't have the energy to get out of bed most days, much less make any attempt at meaningful changes. I was broken and afraid that any additional stress was going to push me over the edge.

Looking back, it's easy to see that forcing myself to get uncomfortable was the best thing I could have done.

It created hope and gave me a place to channel my pain. I know that life is meant to be uncomfortable at times, because the most meaningful personal growth occurs when we are uncomfortable rather than when we are happily complacent. Life is meant to be *lived*—and the best way to truly live is to get outside our comfort zone.

Often. And with enthusiasm.

Creating a legacy for your child or finding your purpose can be uncomfortable. The Grieving Dads mission is a personal example of this. When I first started, it was challenging to leave my comfort zone. Even after I took the first step, I had no idea what would eventually happen. What started as a conscious decision to help others turned into a book and a movement. I didn't want my grief to define me and to become known as a broken-hearted father who never reengaged with life. I wanted to live intentionally, with passion, and reach others along the way. The real game of life isn't just going through the motions but living with purpose and making a positive impact.

Clueless as I was, I jumped out of my comfort zone and embraced the uncomfortable, using it as a distraction and a place for my pain to go. They say where focus goes, energy flows. I focused on helping others, and the universe found a way to help me make my mission a reality.

I have spoken to (literally) thousands of grieving dads over the years, and I can tell you some remarkable stories of guys like you and me who took their pain and did something amazing with it. They created things bigger than themselves and helped many people along the way.

One of those dads, Mike, called me late one Saturday night years ago and started the phone call with something along the lines of "I am sitting here at my kitchen table with a .357 Magnum. I can't do this anymore." As you can imagine, Mike had my undivided attention and I responded swiftly with "Can't do what anymore?" Mike went on to tell me he was an executive at a large corporation, and a few years after losing his child, the job was sucking the life out of him. He needed more. He couldn't keep living life like nothing had ever happened to him. Problem is, something did happen. Something profound. The death of his son.

This wasn't the first time I had spoken to Mike. About a year prior, he had called to thank me for writing the book and for the work I had done with other grieving dads. During that first call, Mike was in good spirits; he was jovial, and overall, he seemed to be in a good place.

Clearly, the mention of the gun on this second call indicated otherwise. Mike revealed to me that he thought he had his pain under control, and as a result, he hadn't looked for any support. Neither had he learned to surrender—he was still trying to fight back, and eventually the pain took over and caught up with him in a big way.

I talked. He listened. He talked. I listened. We were on the phone together for a good while, and we said our goodbyes without any loud noises from his end of the line, thank God.

After that alarming phone call, I didn't hear back from Mike for quite some time. It's not uncommon to get late-night phone calls from dads in despair wanting to tell their story and let out some of their pain. It's also not uncommon for long stretches of time to pass between conversations with grieving dads. However, about five years after that second call with Mike, my phone rang and it showed up as "Mike—.357 Magnum" on my contact list. This time, the call came in the middle of the day, and of course I answered it—elevated blood pressure and all—not knowing what I was going to hear on the other end of the phone.

It was Mike calling to thank me for that discussion we had five years earlier. He said, "I don't know what you said to me that night, but whatever it was, it stopped me from doing the unthinkable." I told him I didn't remember the exact words, but it had something to do with surrendering, seeking help, and then finding something to do that would honor his son.

Everything I am trying to convey in this book.

In the five years since our last conversation, Mike surrendered and got the help he needed. He also made a decision to leave that high-pressure corporate job and do something more meaningful with his life. Mike lives his life with purpose and is now an at-risk inner-city youth counselor, working hard at making a difference in other people's lives. He said he couldn't be happier, and the best part is he knows his son is extremely proud of him.

I have no doubt about that.

Mike's story is one of the many stories from grieving dads I have heard over the years. It may not come to you today or tomorrow, but I challenge each and every one of you to find your "why," your purpose, and to go create your legacy. Your "why" doesn't have to be something that changes the whole world; it needs to be something that changes *your* world and gives you the hope you need to carry on with a meaningful life.

## CHAPTER 8

# THE TRUTH

I'VE SURVIVED ONE hundred percent of my worst days. You *will* do the same.

It's important you know and believe that to be the truth. There may be days where the overwhelming emotional pain, depression, and despair you feel will try to convince you otherwise. It will take you to depths you never thought possible, but you can survive this. The thousands of other grieving dads (and moms) I met over the last thirteen years are proof of that fact.

I am, too.

While surviving one hundred percent of your worst days will be something you achieve as well, you also need to know it doesn't magically happen. You have to embrace the things we've covered in the previous chapters and make the conscious decision to recognize you aren't going back to the "old" you. Your world has changed, forever. If you resist letting go of your pain and getting the help you need, then your truth will become a never-ending spiral of pain and despair.

Make the right choices, and your truth will tell a much better story.

There are, in fact, a whole lot of truths on this journey:

- You *are* a dad.
- Your child loves you and is watching you. Make them proud.
- You will need a passion or a cause to get you out of bed and onto a path that will put hope back into your life.
- You are not alone. There are millions of us dads out there; go find your community. Better yet, create one.
- Some of you will go on to have another child; others will not.
- Some of you will continue to have fertility issues; some of you won't.
- Some of you will distance yourself from others that do have children because it's too hard to watch those around you living the dream you had for yourself.
- This loss will affect everyone close to you in some way.
- Your personal relationships will change, and some of them will not be able to withstand the stress of this loss. It's OK to move on.

- Anger will certainly be a part of this.
- Some of you will try to run from this pain, only to find yourself deeper in despair.
- Some of you will embrace the healing process I laid out in this book.
- If you were the one who passed away, you would want your baby to smile and laugh again anyway. Your baby wants you to do the same.
- You should not feel bad about smiling and laughing again.
- You will stop tolerating bullshit in your life. Don't feel bad about that.
- You will feel peace again in your life, once you do the hard work of surrendering.
- You cannot help anyone else until you have learned to help yourself.
- Some of you will have an awakening and change all aspects of your life that you are not happy with.
- Some of you will turn toward spirituality to get you through this, and others will turn away. Do what is right for you.
- Some of you will build walls around yourself. Fight the urge to do this.
- Fear is going to be a part of this journey. Remember, beyond fear is freedom.
- Going through the fog of despair, you will find clarity on the other side.
- Some of you will simplify your life.
- Dogs make *great* therapists.

- You will always be a work in progress. It's not about perfection, it's about the progress you make. Years later, I am still a work in progress; we all are.
- You will not be the same person you once were.

There are a lot of truths about losing a baby. The ultimate truth is that none of us wants to be remotely aware of what it feels like. But that isn't where we find ourselves. We have no control over it, and it cannot be undone; it will always be a part of our life story.

There is no right way or wrong way to grieve, but there is a right way or wrong way to respond to the grief and pain we all feel. Everyone reading this is at a different point and has different circumstances surrounding their loss. Use this book to guide you along your path and refer to it often to help you seek clarity and make any needed adjustments to your life.

None of us are alone on this journey. Take what you have learned here in this book and go build that legacy in your child's name.

Go make them proud of their dad.

# ADDITIONAL GRIEVING DADS RESOURCES

This is going to be a difficult journey, and I am committed to helping you through this in any way that I can. If you would like to learn more about other child loss support resources that I offer, please scan the QR code below or visit my website at www.GrievingDads.com.

You will find other books I have written, online courses, virtual support, and coaching. Additionally, you will find information about my public speaking and professional training courses designed to help health-care organizations and counselors.

# PLEASE WRITE A REVIEW

If you've found this book helpful, please consider writing a review. Given that I am a self-published author, I don't have the advertising power of a large publisher. The more reviews this book receives, the better it will rank in search results, which means more people will find it.

Honest reviews help other readers find me. It only takes a few minutes, and the review can be as short or long as you would like.

If you would like to leave a review on Amazon.com, search for my book, find the Customer Reviews section, and then click on "Write a customer review." This will help me reach more people who need to read this book.

Thank you!

# ABOUT KELLY FARLEY

Kelly Farley was caught up in the rat race of life when he experienced the loss of two babies over an 18-month period. He lost his daughter, Katie, in October 2004, and his son, Noah, in June 2006.

Like many men, he tried to run from his pain, but he learned the hard way that it will find you. After several years of trying to fight through the pain on his own, he finally acknowledged that he needed help but quickly realized there were few resources for men. He also realized during his journey that society does not feel comfortable with an openly grieving male.

That realization inspired him to write his first book: ***Grieving Dads: To the Brink and Back.*** Kelly has a passion for helping people "pick up the pieces" after a profound life event. Kelly commits his time to developing resources for grieving dads and bringing awareness of the aftermath of losing a child. He currently lives in the suburbs of Chicago with his wife, Christine, and their dog, Cooper, but he often dreams of planning his escape from that city's cold, dark winters.

Kelly Farley
Kelly@GrievingDads.com
(630) 561-5989
www.GrievingDads.com

# ABOUT DAVID DICOLA

David DiCola is a small business owner and freelance writer from Canton, Ohio. As the son of a grieving dad, DiCola's work with Kelly Farley has brought a higher sense of purpose to his writing. David is the author of ***Customer Golf—The Short Game*** as well as several coauthored books across a wide range of subjects. A father of four who is a regular contributor to business publications and blogs, he lives in Munroe Falls, Ohio, with his wife, Anne.

Made in United States
Troutdale, OR
05/28/2024